Discovering
BRASSES AND BRASS
RUBBING

Malcolm Cook

Shire Publications, Tring, Herts.

CONTENTS

Figures 1–4, 6–13, 15–17, 20 reproduced by courtesy of the Victoria and Albert Museum, London. Figures 21 and 22 by courtesy of R. H. Elms.

Copyright © 1971 by Shire Publications. 'Discovering Brasses' first published August 1967. Subsequent editions and impressions in December 1967, March 1968, July 1968, March 1969, September 1969, September 1970. This fifth edition published August 1971. ISBN 0 85263040 9.

INTRODUCTION

Of all the monuments to be seen in the cathedrals and churches of Britain perhaps the least recognised are the medieval engraved memorial brasses. This neglect is not surprising when it is realized that brasses are generally to be found in the most inaccessible spots—under pews and mats, behind the organ and, in one instance, on the steeple roof.

In the last decade, however, there has been an increased interest in brasses, partly due to references in the press, but also to the discovery, by interior decorators in particular, that facsimile representations of brasses make excellent wall hangings.

Nevertheless, whilst people are ready enough to appreciate the pictorial qualities of these reproductions, there is a wealth of colourful history and interest behind the purely visual aspect of which they are not generally aware. Besides giving us a pictorial history of the development of armour, civilian fashions and ecclesiastical vestments from the thirteenth to the end of the seventeenth centuries, memorial brasses form a valuable, indeed a unique, commentary on day-to-day life in medieval England.

All classes of society are commemorated: bishops, knights, ladies, city burghers, monks and servants. As brasses could be made in almost any size—ranging from a small half-effigy with a two-line inscription to life-sized figures accompanied by canopy work—they were within the financial reach of a large cross-section of the community. This is underlined by the fact that the vast majority of persons commemorated by them are the possessors of names absolutely unknown to history. Whereas the achievements of the aristocracy are recorded in art, literature, architecture and heraldry, we should know little of the daily life of the middle classes, were it not for their brasses. A new light, for example, is thrown upon the Wars of the Roses when we find that in spite of troublesome times, brasses became more and more common, from which we can deduce that the struggles of the rival factions had little influence on the peaceful middle classes, who were all the time moving into the towns and steadily increasing in wealth and importance.

That is why in this guide I shall deal mainly with a representative selection of brasses in the southern half of England. In this area were concentrated the majority of the medieval market towns that traded with France and the Low Countries, and consequently the area is rich in brasses of English and Continental origin.

1 Sir John d'Abernoun, 1277, Stoke
d'Abernon, Surrey

2 Sir Roger de Trumpington, 1289,
Trumpington, Cambs.

THE MANUFACTURE OF BRASSES

The use of engraved brass plates as memorials to the dead appears to have been introduced into England from the Low Countries during the late thirteenth century as an improvement on the incised slabs of stone used previously. Britain's geographical separation from the rest of the Continent has left it in possession of some 4,000 figure brasses. Although this is only the remnant of what must have been a very large total—their numbers having been reduced by the religious upheavals of the Reformation, Puritan iconoclasts, metal thieves, neglect and vandalism—it is ten times more than the brasses remaining on the Continent, where memorials had also to withstand plunder and destruction by invading armies. In France, during the Revolution of 1789, sacrilege and the destruction of brasses were rife, and if one assessed the counter-sinkings of brasses in British churches and compared the number with those in Flanders, the number in Flanders would probably be greater.

The change from stone to brass

The earliest known surviving brass is not in England at all but in the Church of St. Andrew, Verden, near Hanover in Germany and it commemorates Bishop Ysowilpe. It is dated 1231. Similarly, the finest brass of Flemish workmanship, of rectangular design, also occurs on the Continent at Ringsted in Denmark. It represents King Eric Menved and his queen Ingeborg and is dated 1319.

However, in order to be able to appreciate the aesthetic qualities of early English brasses, it is necessary to consider the incised stones which preceded brass plates as memorials, and which exercised such an influence on the art of the originators of the brasses at Verden and Ringsted, who were later to establish their craft in England.

The incised slab is derived from the stone lid which covered the coffin and which was at first carved with an inscription or motif. Later in the twelfth century, a portrait of the deceased was used. This was further enhanced by carving the design of the figure in semi-relief which led to evolution of the figure carved in full-relief. Because of the expense of importing Tournai stone and Italian marble these types of memorial were not very popular in Britain, and for every thousand slabs that survive on the Continent, there are only a hundred remaining in Britain. On the other hand, for every hundred brasses extant abroad there are one thousand examples to be seen in Britain. It follows that in this country the craft of brass engraving was able to develop independent of competition and influence from abroad. Brass plate was more durable, more easily worked than stone, and gave more opportunity for detailed engraving. Thus, although both crafts achieve the same degree of completeness, their separate development, due mainly to geographical circumstances, was inevitable.

The cost of brass memorials

Now let us consider the manufacture of the brass itself, from the time the order was given to the engraver, up to the inscribing of the date of death on the plate, maybe a quarter of a century later.

Wills and contracts entered into with the makers of brasses and their agents provide interesting information about the cost of brasses. Philip, Lord D'Arcy (died 1399) directed in his will that "a marbell stone be placed over my tomb, to be worked with two images of laten, to the likeness of myselfe and my wyf Elizabeth of the price of £10." Latten was the alloy from which brasses were made.

When the order had been placed the contract had to be prepared. An extremely good example of a contract for a brass in the form of a cross and two tombs is given below; it is also interesting because it mentions certain side-aspects of the manufacture of brasses. However, because the original document is in French, and is lengthy and archaic, a *precis* version is given.

"A contract for two tombs, between Thomas Leigh, merchant, and Cornelius Hermansone, acting on behalf of William, Lord Sandys, with Arnold Hermansone, native of Amsterdam, established at Aire in Artois, was proved before a notary at Antwerp on Monday, 1st March, 1536. One tomb was to be of Antoing stone[1], eight Flemish feet long by four and half broad and four and a quarter high; the slab to be inlaid with a cross of copper, red and white, and dates also in brass three inches wide. The other tomb . . . The tombs to be delivered at Antwerp, in all respects conforming to the design given, under a penalty of ten livres of great Flemish money if they are not delivered within seven months and thence shipped to England; the said Arnold to go over to Basingstoke and finish them off properly. For this, he would receive thirty livres and also the expenses of his journey and stay in England."

Making the brass plates

Once the design had been worked out and a contract drawn up

[1] 'Antoing stone' (from a parish a few miles above Tournai, on the Scheldt) is almost black.

between the parties, the engraver could begin inscribing the plate according to the instructions given him.

Brasses consist of two distinct elements. There are firstly the plates of metal or latten on which the figure of the deceased was portrayed, and secondly the indent, or countersunk stone slab, in which the engraved plate was set flush by means of metal rivets and black pitch.

Latten was composed mainly of copper and zinc, other metals being present in very small proportions.

Because the process of rolling metals was only introduced in the eighteenth century, an ingenious system involving water-powered hammers was used to beat the metal into small sheets. Nevertheless, although sufficient quantities of sheet metal to meet the demand could be produced using this system, the quality obtained was not all that could be desired. Clearly the machine-hammers of the fourteenth to eighteenth century could not be expected to turn out sheets of very accurate width and thickness, and this is proved by the uneven size of many early brasses.

Engravers did not necessarily cast their own plates, and their location was determined more by the market for their work than by the source of their materials. The cost of raw materials could be passed on to the person ordering the brass, and so immediate access to stone quarries or mining centres was not important, emphasis being more on immediate access to the client. Thus engraving centres tended to appear wherever there were thriving centres of trade, for example, at Antwerp and Bruges in the Low Countries, in East Anglia and London in England.

Engraving the brass

Latten could be decorated in many ways. Firstly, the sheet could be engraved in its entirety. Secondly, the outline of the figure of the deceased could be inserted into an indent. As a third possibility, only certain portions of the design would be cut in brass, for example, the hands and inscriptions, whilst the rest of the memorial constituted an incised slab. This last type is especially pleasing, combining as it does the best qualities inherent in both brass and stone.

The "burin" or chisel used for engraving the design in the metal could be used in a number of ways. A popular method abroad was to cut away the surface of the metal leaving the design raised in semi-relief.

Enamelling

As another variation, colour could be added, in the form of enamel inlay. This was an expensive form of decoration and is not to be found on many English brasses. There is an interesting

7

theory, put forward by Herbert Haines, the nineteenth century authority on monumental brasses, that the craft may have developed from the practice of making what are called "Limoges enamels," which came into fashion in Europe during the twelfth century. His hypothesis is that the Limoges enamels were derived from the 'cloissonée' work of the Chinese, whereby a metal surface is covered with a pattern of ridges, the space between them being filled with a variety of coloured preparations and then being highly polished. He then goes on to assume— and this is quite reasonable—that if the enamels were laid on a prepared surface of latten, the craftsman might easily see fit to omit fixing the ridges to act as separators for the various coloured enamels used, and instead to carve the design in semi-relief. From the plate carved in semi-relief, the brass as we know it, without any enamel embellishments at all, might have evolved as a cheaper form of memorial which was more durable and less liable to chip or crack than those with enamel inlays. Unfortunately, however, there is insufficient evidence in the form of enamelled brasses or documentary records to prove that there is any direct link between the two crafts of engraving and enamelling.

Indenting

So, when the engraved brass was complete it had to be delivered and set in position. We know from information contained in the Halyburton ledger that about one-third of the expense of imported brasses was taken up by transport costs. Indeed, the Basingstoke contract previously mentioned bears this out by making provision for the cost of the engraver's journey to England and his stay to be borne by the client. It should be remembered, however, that the task of the monumental mason of the old days was not an easy one. His wagon had to carry large stone tombs and his horses had to be strong and healthy if they were to pull such loads. Although it was obviously cheaper to use local stone for the tomb itself, we find that blue Tournai stone was much used in the north of England as a base for memorials instead of the local Yorkshire stone, so the cost cannot have deterred the majority of persons ordering brasses. This conforms with the general theory that it was mainly the members of the affluent middle class who were the brass engravers' main source of income.

The engraved plate was then set into the indent that had been carved for it. This was simply a matter of lowering the brass into the indent, which had been filled with pitch, and allowing the brass to settle in the required position. In later brasses metal rivets were used to secure the plates.

Although brasses aim to commemorate the persons they depict they are not attempts at portraiture. This might at first seem rather surprising, but when it is remembered that the task of actually drawing the design for a brass was usually entrusted to the engraver himself, it is not unusual to find that a characteristic 'face' developed which was used on all brasses emanating from his workshop. Thus schools of brass-engraving can be identified in different parts of the country.

Nevertheless, we do sometimes come across examples of brasses that have been 'personalized'. The beard of Sir William Tendring (1408) at Stoke by Nayland, Suffolk is undoubtedly an attempt at capturing a feature which contrasted with the current fashion of the times. At Ingoldmells, Lincs, William Palmer (1520), a cripple, is shown 'with ye stylt'. The pet dog Terri is identified in the brass to Alice Cassy at Deerhurst, Glos.

So, brasses are valuable to us not so much as records of particular persons or their personal idiosyncrasies but as records of the classes of persons represented. Apart from military effigies, the majority of persons depicted were of the middle class—the traders and merchants on whom the rest of the country depended for its prosperity.

In addition to being rich in brasses of a middle-class nature, England has many brasses to the aristocracy, the landed gentry, and the titled. These people were the defenders of the faith, who fought in the Crusades (as well as amongst themselves) and who owned estates covering very large areas.

The evolution of defensive armour was determined by two inter-relating factors. Firstly, the development of a new weapon by an aggressor had to be countered with improved armour worn by his opponent, if he was not to die on the battlefield. At the same time the need for agility in attack and retreat restricted the amount of armour that could be carried in defence. This conflict —the need for mobility against the instinct for self-preservation— is very clearly depicted on the monumental brasses of mediaeval warriors. Then, with the introduction of hand-guns and cannon the pace of battle quickened considerably, and consequently, as the effective range between armies increased, the need for a head-to-toe and elaborate covering of armour diminished.

Brasses, showing the styles of armour worn from the Middle Ages until after the Civil War, can be arranged, broadly speaking, into six periods. These are the thirteenth century, the two halves of the fourteenth century, the fifteenth century, and the Tudor period covering the sixteenth and the early seventeenth centuries.

The thirteenth century brasses

The earliest brass in England is that of Sir John d'Abernoun (1277) at Stoke d'Abernon in Surrey, fig. 1 on page 4. It is a fine brass, measuring seventy-eight inches in length, and surrounded by the following inscription in Norman French: *Sire: John: Daubernon: Chivalier: Gist: Icy: Dieu: de: Sa: Alme: Eyt: Mercy.*

This is the only example of a brass where the principal figure holds to his chest a lance such as was commonly used in jousting tournaments. A pennant flies from its arrow-like blade. A playful-looking lion grasps the butt-end of the spear, rather as a kitten would hold a knitting-needle between its teeth. Slung by a leather strap or *guige* from his right shoulder is his shield which bears a chevron, the same armorial device as the pennant. Sir John wears a hood or *coif-de-mailles* and a shirt of mail (*hawberk*), the sleeves of which extend to form mittens. His hands are clasped in prayer, the traditional pose for both brasses and stone monuments of a military nature. Over his suit of mail is seen the typical *surcoat*, girded at the waist, which was perhaps intended to protect the wearer against the discomfort of wearing hot mail in summertime, or to protect it against damp, which would rust it. Over the surcoat is slung his sword belt, fastened by an intricate series of leather thongs. It makes his sword look extremely heavy and unwieldy. Its hilt is cruciform, the pommel spherical and its cross-guards nearly straight. The surcoat is parted at the front to reveal the *chausses* or mail stockings. To these are attached *genouillères* or decorated leather kneecaps, and strapped to his ankles are pointed *pryck* spurs.

Traces of blue enamel are still apparent on the shield, emphasising the bold contrasting design of this magnificent brass, which must have been a rare sight to behold in its heyday, brazen and radiant, as it is even now.

In the second oldest brass in Britain, that of Sir Roger de Trumpington (1289) at Trumpington, near Cambridge, fig. 2 on page 4, there are many similarities in the style of engraving. There are, however, two or three marked differences. Firstly, the feet are crossed. In the past this has led many writers on the subject of brasses and stone effigies to suppose that the 'legs crossed' attitude indicated that the person depicted was a crusader. In this case, there is evidence that Sir Roger did actually take part in Prince Edward's expedition to Palestine in 1270. However, in the majority of instances it can be proved that the subjects of most cross-legged figures of brass and stone never set foot in the Holy Land.

Secondly, Sir Roger's feet rest on a hound, as opposed to the lion at the feet of Sir John. Here again, some writers see a deep significance, assuming that one knight died fighting, whilst the

3 *Sir Robert de Bures, 1302,*
Acton, Suffolk

4 *Sir Robert de Septvans, c. 1306,*
Chartham, Kent

other passed away when the country was at peace. Although the lion can be taken as a symbol of courage and manliness, the hound, or more appropriately the *levrier*, was the symbol of his master's sport, and as such was in keeping with the chivalrous quality of the rest of the brass.

The third main contrast between these two brasses is in the styles of mail worn. It is contended by some authorities that there is no direct archaeological evidence to show that two types of chain mail were being manufactured during the thirteenth century. Nevertheless, two styles of mail are evident in a comparison of the above two brasses. Sir John d'Abernoun wears "linked" mail: Sir Roger de Trumpington "banded" mail. It could be that the two methods of representation were employed by different engravers to suggest the complicated nature of the mail ringlets. Both methods are equally effective.

Chain mail, as a complete defence, was worn up to about 1320. The brasses to two unidentified knights, one of the Fitzralphs, at Pebmarsh, Essex, and a Bacon at Gorleston, Suffolk, mark the beginning of a transition towards the increased use of plate armour as a complement to chain mail.

Early fourteenth century brasses

The early fourteenth century from about 1320 to 1350 is characterized by the increased use of plate defences, culminating in the elimination of mail as protective outerwear for the body. It was still the main form of protection for the neck, however, which had to be free to move.

There are a number of brasses characteristic of this period, the majority of which are to be found in the southern half of England. Two of these brasses are of foreign workmanship— Sir Robert de Septvans (c. 1306) at Chartham, Kent, fig. 4, and Sir John de Northwode (c. 1330) at Minster on the Isle of Sheppey, Kent. It is thought that both of these may be of French origin, owing to certain peculiarities of style which cannot directly be related to English workmanship on brasses and slabs.

Perhaps the most characteristic English brass of the period is that at Westley Waterless, Cambs. Here lie Sir John de Creke and his lady (1325), fig. 5. His short surcoat, sometimes termed a *cyclas*, reveals a padded garment, the *haketon*, intended to protect the body from the chafing of the heavy mail shirt or *hawberk*, which is also visible. Over the hawberk can be seen the *pourpoint*, a fringed skirt rather similar to that worn by Roman legionaries. It is inset with rosettes. The *coif-de-mailles* has given way to the armoured helmet or *bascinet*, with its pendant mail neck defence or visor. Roundels, shaped in the form of a lion's head, act as shoulder guards. The spurs are of rowel form,

5 Sir John de Creke and wife, 1325, Westley Waterless, Cambs.

wheel-like, whilst the sword is much the same as that seen in thirteenth century brasses. The knight holds his shield in the same way as Sir John d'Abernoun, slung from his right shoulder by the *guige* and facing forwards. It can be seen that in earlier examples, the shield was sometimes shewn in half view—the heraldic 'artist's licence', which preserved the artistic composition of the figure and did not disturb the line.

Comparing this brass to that of Sir John d'Abernoun II (1327), there is little doubt that both are by the same hand even though there are certain minor differences in detail. Both footrests are lions. The pourpoint in the d'Abernoun brass is more ornate than the Creke example, yet the roundels are more elaborate in the latter. A beard, partly concealed, is evidence of the new fashion for men at that time.

The first half of the fourteenth century as represented on military brasses closes with the fine brass at Elsing, Norfolk (1347). This is an interesting brass because the main figure, Sir Hugh Hastings, is surrounded by a series of panels depicting armed weepers and religious scenes. Among many interesting details shown are iron throat guards, *gorgets*, helmet visors, *pourpointerie* or rivet studded thigh defences and the *chapelle-de-fer* or wide-brimmed war-hat of Almeric, Lord St. Amand. The brass is surrounded by a canopy and is extremely impressive in spite of the fact that it has been much despoiled.

The Elsing brass and others at Bowers Gifford and Wimbish in Essex illustrate variations in armour styles and thus are accepted by some authorities as marking the transition (from 1345 to 1355) between the two halves of the fourteenth century, rather than the beginning or end of either period.

Late fourteenth century brasses

During the sixty years ending in 1410, covering the reigns of Edward III, Richard II and Henry IV, armour achieved a more uniform design; variations in style do not occur so often. This could, however, mean that as the craft of brass-engraving became more widespread and schools of engraving came into existence, there was no longer the time, nor the demand, to represent the same degree of varying detail that typified thirteenth century brasses. So although armour continued to evolve, we cannot say with real certainty how universal such changes in style were.

The most consistent feature of this period was the adoption of the tight-fitting *jupon*, successor to the shortened loose surcoat, whilst the bascinet and mail neck defence or *camail* were retained much in their old form. Other aspects of armour were much improved upon: a metal studded belt, the *baldric*, which

6 William de Aldeburgh, c. 1360,
Aldborough, Yorks.

7 Sir John Harpedon, 1438,
Westminster Abbey

15

succeeded the cumbersome sword belt with its straps and thongs, was adopted. The hawberk becomes shorter eventually to be replaced by the *cuirass* or breast-plate, made either of plate or of toughened leather which had been boiled in oil. Leather also takes the place of mail *chausses* and sleeves, as a lighter and more malleable undergarment. A small dagger, the *misericord*, became popular and was attached to the baldric on the wearer's right side. The shield appears gradually to have fallen into disuse through the increasing use of plate armour. The last brass to show a shield carried adjacent to the body is that of William de Aldeburgh (c. 1360), fig. 6 on page 15, yet this is the earliest brass to show the misericord.

There are many examples of brasses of this period. Unfortunately the majority are not in the best condition, having been torn up and mutilated during the Reformation and the Civil War. Choice examples are rare. Cobham, Kent, has several nice examples to be seen side by side in the chancel of the church. There is an interesting one at Drayton Beauchamp in Bucks. The 'bell-tassels' attached to the leg armour of Thomas Cheyne (1368), who appears on the cover of this book, would surely have announced his presence to an enemy on the field of battle! Similar rivets, probably securing an inner lining of metal strips, are also seen on the leather leg-armour of Sir Miles de Stapleton (1364), on the brass which was formerly at Ingham, Norfolk.

In both of these brasses the skirted jupon of the Elsing brass has been superseded by the tight-fitting jupon of leather, covered with satin or velvet. Often this was decorated with heraldic devices as in the case of William de Aldeburgh, fig. 6. The emblazoned jupon was the forerunner of the heraldic *tabard*, a loose garment, with wide sleeves, worn by many fifteenth century knights.

The fifteenth century

From 1410 until the end of the fifteenth century the soldiers represented are all wearing complete plate armour. Mail seems to have been discontinued as a form of protective undergarment covering the whole body—it was, however, still used as an additional protection for the most exposed parts. Thus the camail seen in the brass to Thomas Cheyne has by now been completely superseded by the gorget, which first made its appearance on brasses some sixty years earlier, suggesting that both forms of neck defences were being used concurrently. The bascinet, having become more pointed during the fourteenth century, now takes on a globular form. The rest of the armour is much the same as that of the preceding period, except from the waist down where a series of narrow overlapping plates, *taces*,

8 Sir Peter Courtenay, 1409, Exeter Cathedral

were attached. The roundel as an armpit guard also becomes more pronounced, altering its shape until by the end of the century it has adopted an almost rectangular form.

The portrait of Sir John Harpedon (1438), fig. 7 on page 15, is a fine example of a military brass of this time. Of interest are the exceptional number of taces—ten altogether—protecting the midriff, the almost rectangular roundels, and the four shields in the corners of the tomb. From these we know that Sir John's third wife was Lady Joan de Cobham; he was her fifth husband. Contemporary records give us reason to believe that her fourth husband, Sir John Oldcastle, condemned as a heretic and burnt at the stake in 1417, was the prototype of Shakespeare's character Falstaff. The entire figure of Sir John Harpedon has a beautifully streamlined effect which was later destroyed by the development of highly exaggerated elbow pieces and thigh protectors. This brass is very clean cut, having suffered little damage. The rowel spurs, which are usually the first parts of a brass to show damage, are in perfect condition. Part of the cloth mantling which should hang from the helmet on which his head rests is missing. A similar helm is seen in the thirteenth century brass to Sir Roger de Trumpington, fig. 2 on page 4, and in the wonderful canopied brass to Sir Peter Courtenay (1409) in Exeter Cathedral, fig. 8 on page 17.

There is some doubt, however, as to the actual date of the Harpedon brass and it is suggested that it might have been executed 1425-1440, the armour on the effigy conforming to that period. The solution is probably that Sir John followed a by no means uncommon custom and had his effigy engraved during his lifetime. Mill Stephenson gives 1438 as the date for Sir John's death.

About 1445 a change in style of armour is apparent. Foreign armouries and workshops began to exert an influence on the style of English armour, which was to mean a gradual decline in its individuality. This is reflected in brasses which lose the neat symmetrical and clean cut appearance inherent in the Harpedon brass. This is partly due to the fact that Milanese armour is not easy to reduce to linear form; exaggerations and inaccuracies tend to occur. Obviously the three-dimensional stone representation managed to convey this new style in a more dignified manner. On brass the old idea of a recumbent figure seems to have been forgotten, poses and three-quarter views becoming more popular. Footrests in the form of lions and hounds tend to disappear, to be replaced by small mounds sprouting grass or flowers.

Nevertheless, although English armour (and consequently the design of brasses) was being affected by the influences of Milan

9 John Teringham, 1484,
Tyringham, Bucks

10 Sir Thomas Bullen, 1538,
Hever, Kent

and the gothic school of the Colmans at Augsburg, there appears to have been a direct development from the traditional style of English armour, which persisted alongside the foreign-influenced styles until about 1500. It will be recalled that the tabard was the direct successor of the emblazoned jupon of the previous period.

Tabard-clad knights are to be seen on many of our brasses. The brass at Tyringham shows the tabard most clearly. Here John Teringham (1484), fig. 9, is seen with his feet resting on a hound footrest and a long inscription. The nature of the garment is clear—a loose kind of vest worn over the armour, protecting it from the elements, without restricting the movements of the wearer. This brass shows the visored *sallet* helmet which had replaced the bascinet as armoured headgear. The *pauldrons*, or exaggerated elbow guards in the gothic style, protrude from under the tabard.

19

The gothic style generally succeeded the Italian style of armour. The latter was characterized by the armour of the left elbow being reinforced and exaggerated. This is well illustrated in the brass to John Daundelyon (1445) at Margate, Kent.

At the same time the gothic style began to deteriorate, the pointed forms becoming more rounded. For instance the pointed sollerts of John Teringham are already quite rounded although they have not developed into the broad-toed *sabbatons* of the next century. In the brass to Edward Sulyard and his wife (c. 1495) at High Laver, Essex, the rounded sabbatons are seen. The taces or plated strips have almost disappeared to reveal a mail skirt over the leg armour. Buckled to the lowermost tace are two *tuilles*. Generally these were small plates for protecting the legs in addition to the mail skirt which was now becoming more exposed. However, in this case they are somewhat exaggerated in length. This brass can be described as transitional, from the fifteenth century into the sixteenth.

The sixteenth century

During the sixteenth century brass engraving in England reached its lowest ebb. This is not to say that foreign armour styles were responsible, because continental brasses do not exhibit the general ugliness and poor workmanship of English examples at this time. Perhaps the Continental engravers were more able to cope with the intricacies and idiosyncracies of continental armour. In England, however, lack of knowledge of the complicated nature of such armour tended to emphasize the general confusion of brass designing.

Poor design is evident in the brass to Sir Thomas Brooke (1529) at Cobham, Kent. The legs are out of proportion to the rest of the body. Shading has been introduced—lavishly, as if to suggest a third dimension—but one feels it betrays a certain lack of confidence and understanding for the craft of brass-engraving, which is essentially a single-plane art. The most marked feature of the gothic style—the breastplate, with its pointed *tapul* or ridge—has been allowed to continue into the sixteenth century, when it had been abandoned before the transition period, represented by the Sulyard brass.

Nevertheless, although the general level of brass-designing had reached its lowest ebb at this time, there are two or three nice examples of intrinsically English brasses of this period. Sir Thomas Bullen (1538) at Hever, Kent, fig. 10 on page 9, is a fine knight wearing the insignia of the Garter. His mantle drops to his feet which, rather surprisingly, rest on an animal (a griffin). The engraving is firm, and the lines are sure. The Garter is worn below the left knee.

11 Sir Peter Leigh, 1527, Winwick, Lancs.

The brass to Sir Peter Leigh (1527) at Winwick, Lancashire, fig. 11, is interesting. The deceased wears a priest's chasuble over his armour, rather similar to a tabard. In this case the vestment has been decorated with his arms, and his wife also wears a decorated mantle. Sir Peter was a knight before becoming a priest after the death of his wife.

Tabards were worn during this period right up to about 1550. Sir Ralph Verney (1547) at Aldbury, Herts, is a good representation of a sixteenth century knight wearing this type of garment which has not altered appreciably for a century. Again, the wife wears an emblazoned mantle, fig. 12.

12 Sir Ralph Verney and wife, 1547, Aldbury, Herts.

After 1550, helmets and leg-armour seem to be omitted and one gets the impression that suits of armour were retained and worn for occasions of pomp and ceremony, rather than for actual use in armed confrontations. (England was at this time essentially a naval power.) In the Carolian brass to John Pen (1641) and his wife at Penn in Bucks, John is wearing knee-high leather boots and a falling collar in the puritan style. The tuilles have disappeared, to be replaced by *lamboys* of similar form, but much larger and attached to the breastplate.

After the Civil War, armour, except for a breastplate, ceased to be worn as a protection. The need for agility on the field of

13 *Richard Torrington and wife,*
   1356, Berkhamsted, Herts.

14 *Richard Beauforest,*
   last abbot of Dor-
   chester, Oxon.,
   16th century.

battle and the perfection of the arquebus and musket meant that
heavy armour soon became obsolete. Nevertheless, when it is
remembered that the pack carried by the "Tommy" of the First
World War, three hundred years later, easily outweighed the
armour of any soldier of previous centuries, it is fitting to finish
by mentioning the brass to Lt. Col. Harry Addison (1915), at
Sledmore in Yorkshire.

CIVILIAN COSTUME BRASSES

The majority of British brasses represent the ordinary undistinguished middle class civilian. Although some writers prefer to separate ladies into a distinct class from civilians and male costume brasses, I have included them here, treating traders and scholars as a separate category to be dealt with later.

Male civilian costume in the fourteenth century

The earliest brasses of civilians, male and female, are to be found in the Home Counties. At Berkhamsted, in Hertfordshire, there is a simple memorial to Richard Torrington and his wife (1356), fig. 13, in which the man wears a long loose gown with close sleeves and a collar buttoned right up to the neck. His wife wears a modest *cote-hardie*, a sort of tunic, reaching to the feet. Her chest and throat are covered and she wears delicate pointed shoes rather like her husband's. They hold hands.

The small brass to an unknown lady at Pitstone, in Buckinghamshire (c. 1310), fig. 21, page 39, shows her wearing a loose flowing cote-hardie, which hangs from the shoulders. The head is covered with a light veil or *covrechie*, which falls to the shoulders. Incidentally, this much-pitted memorial is probably the earliest brass of a female figure so far recorded in Britain.

In the brass to Robert Braunche and his wives (1364) at King's Lynn, Norfolk, fig. 15, a different style, though pertaining to the same period, is seen. The dress is more elaborate and is shorter than the tunic at Berkhamsted. The sleeves end at the elbows instead of extending to the wrists, and have long *tippets*—or yard-long lengths attached to them. It is generally thought that this type of dress was worn by the wealthier merchants, for it is also seen in the brass at Taplow to Nicholas d'Aumberdene (c. 1350), fig. 16 on page 28, who was a member of the Fishmongers' Company. Both this and the King's Lynn example are brasses of foreign workmanship, which would add weight to this assumption.

Female costume in the fourteenth century

The similiarity of the woman's cote-hardie to the man's tunic will be noticed. However, after about 1360, changes in women's headgear became apparent whilst menswear remained much as it had been. Sometimes the hair was enclosed by a *nebulé* or zig-zag head-dress, as worn by the wife of Sir Reginald de Malyns, (1385), Chinnor, Oxon. The reticulated head-dress, a kind of hair-net studded with jewels, came in about 1370 and lasted for

15 Robert Braunche and wives, 1364, King's Lynn, Norfolk

25

MONARCH	DATE OF ACCESSION	FASHION PERIODS	MALE head	MALE rest	FEMALE head-dress	FEMALE rest
Edward II	1307	1300–1370	long beard and moustache	long tunic	kerchief	cote-hardie and kirtle
Edward III	1327					
Richard II	1377	1370–1415	short hair	short tunic	reticulated	sideless cote-hardie
Henry IV	1399	1370–1420	cleanshaven and short hair		nebulé	gown and mantle
Henry V	1413	1400–1450		long baggy tunic	crespigne	
Henry VI	1422	1420–1480	cleanshaven and long hair	long gown	horned	
Edward IV	1461	1460–1490			butterfly	fur linings
Edward V	1483					
Richard III	1483					
Henry VII	1485	1480–1550		wide belt	dog-kennel	sash
Henry VIII	1509					
Edward VI	1547					
Jane and Mary	1553	1550–1600	moustache and beard	padding	French bonnet	short sleeves
Elizabeth I	1558			ruffs		
James I	1603	1600+		short cloak	Puritan	ruffs and farthingale
Charles I	1625		moustache and curls	knee boots		

some fifty years being contemporary with the nebulé style. Also about 1370 the sideless cote-hardie was introduced, allowing greater freedom of movement; rather like the knight's tabard, it was cut away at the sides.

Widows wore a costume much like the customary garment of a nun in our time. A fine example is the large English brass to Alianore de Bohun (1399) in Westminster Abbey, fig. 17. on page 28. She was the wife of the Duke of Gloucester, who lies buried elsewhere in the abbey, and she is seen wearing the traditional vestments of a widow, the most distinctive of which was the pleated barbe or gorget worn above or below the chin. The costume of widows, which remained unchanged until the sixteenth century, is repeated in the brass to Dame Susan Kyngeston at Shalstone, Bucks. (1540). Her hair is covered by a wimple and she wears a ring of sorrow, to commemorate the death of her husband.

Changes in fashion in the fifteenth and sixteenth century

At the beginning of the fifteenth century, both men's and women's clothing changed, but certain characteristics—baggy sleeves, long cloaks and tunics with fur linings—were retained. Women's hairstyles continued to change. Between 1400 and 1450 the *crespigne* head-dress was conspicuous. The horned head-dress, developed from the reticulated style, came in twenty years after the crespigne style. It was made by extending the tresses of the hair over the ears and placing them over an embroidered kerchief.

During the period 1460 to 1490, shoes became more rounded —mainly due to the passing of an Act of Parliament in 1463 prohibiting the wearing of shoes with points more than two inches long. Gentlemen wore rosaries and *gypcières*, or pouches suspended from the belt. The *anelace*, a dagger carried by the well-to-do civilian of the fourteenth century, disappears around this time. By 1485, the broad shoes introduced after the 1463 Act, have become more sober, as a result of the passing of another Act, this time forbidding shoes with toes of more than six inches in breadth.

The head-dress now in vogue was the butterfly, made by brushing the hair back into nets and extending the veil on wire wings. This style, which was perhaps the most becoming of all those depicted on brass, is seen in the brass to Lady Say (1473) at Broxbourne, Herts. She also wears a heraldic mantle, with close-fitting sleeves and an expensive-looking jewelled necklace.

New fashions were introduced about 1490. The emphasis seems to have been on linings and gowns which were belted at the waist. Women also appear to have followed this style, but used

16 *Nicholas d'Aumberdene,*
1350, Taplow, Bucks

17 *Alianore de Bohun, 1399,*
Westminster Abbey

longer sashes. The dog-kennel or pedimental hairstyle seems to
have been the mode from 1480 until about 1550. Examples of
this particularly English style are to be seen at Harefield, Middx
(1537, 1540) and West Malling, Kent (1543).

In 1550 false sleeves and shoulder paddings became popular
with men. Ruffs at the neck and wrists are used on women's
clothes, which are now a trifle less modest than in previous times.
A petticoat or underskirt is sometimes revealed. The head-dress

of the day, which persisted until at least 1600, was the French bonnet, a simple cap and veil with a horse-shoe front. Good examples of this style are to be seen at Staplehurst in Kent (1580) and in St. Martin's, Canterbury (1587).

During Queen Elizabeth's reign, and indeed up to the death of Charles I in 1649, male costume changed little, although during Charles I's reign, ruffs and frills were replaced by collars and cuffs, jackboots were introduced and a short cloak was sometimes worn, by younger sons especially.

Women appeared in hats—tall, broad-rimmed and puritanical. Skirts and bodices became more shaped, folds in dresses becoming creased pleats. The farthingale or hooped skirt is seen in the brass to the wife of John Pen (1641) at Penn in Bucks.

After 1640 brass-engraving ceased as an art. Although there are a few effigies of the late seventeenth and the eighteenth century, they are not of any consequence, and do not serve to tell us anything of costumes that we do not already know from contemporary printed sources.

Nevertheless the changing fashions, both male and female, of the preceding three centuries do serve as an accurate method of dating brasses. In some cases fashions overlap and the table on page 26 shows the different periods and styles of male and female fashions.

18 Mark at the feet of John Fortey, 1458, Northleach, Glos.

19 Footrest, John Taylor, c. 1490, Northleach, Glos.

OCCUPATIONS, TRADES AND VOCATIONS

Up to this point we have considered only military effigies and those of civilians, who, although they represent the middle classes, do not represent any specific trade or occupation. At least, on examination of their brasses, there is nothing specific to connect them to any particular employment and so we must content ourselves with appreciation of their costume and dress.

Merchant's trade-marks

The representation of merchants and traders on brass is interesting because although the costume is much the same as that of the civilian, there are certain indications of the particular occupation of the person depicted, such as the merchant's mark to be found on many English brasses. These were used initially as business marks, but then came to be unofficially incorporated into family crests. Thus, they can be allied to the mason's mark on a building, denoting authorship and profession. The wreath at the feet of John Fortey (1458), Northleach, Glos., fig. 18 on page 29, encloses his mark. The initials I and F are the initials of his name; the remainder of the device is his trade-mark. The mark of John Taylor, woolman (c. 1490), fig. 19, in the same church, is composed of three shepherd's crooks and a woolpack, on which stands a sheep.

In addition to personal marks many brasses were engraved with the arms of the great merchant companies to which the deceased had belonged.

The wide diversity of occupations carried on in and around London during the fifteenth and sixteenth centuries is evident from the list of brasses given below:

MERCHANT COMPANY	NAME	DATE	LOCATION
Merchant Adventurers	Thos. Pownder	1525	Ipswich (Christchurch Museum), Suffolk
Brewers	Roger James	1591	All Hallows by the Tower, London
Butchers	Thos. Adams	1626	Swanbourne, Bucks
Carpenters	Thos. Edmonds	1619	Horsell, Surrey
Drapers	Sir G. Monox	1543	Walthamstow, Essex
Fishmongers	Nicholas d'Aumberdene	c. 1350	Taplow, Bucks
Goldsmiths	— Hanbury	1593	Datchet, Bucks

Grocers	Thos. White	1610	Finchley, Middx
Haberdashers	Unknown	c. 1580	Faversham, Kent
Ironmongers	John Carre	1570	Stondon Massey, Essex
Mercers	John Carman	1508	Worstead, Norfolk
Merchant Taylors	Rich. Fynche	1640	Dunstable, Beds
Salters	Andrew Evyngar	1533	All Hallows by the Tower, London
Skinners	Wm. Shosmith	1479	Mereworth, Kent
Staple of Calais	Ant. Cave	1558	Chicheley, Bucks
Stationers	John Daye	1584	Little Bradley, Suffolk

Brasses to wool merchants

During the thirteenth century the Cistercian monks had become the greatest wool merchants in England. By the sixteenth century this trade had expanded to such a degree that it formed the most lucrative export of the country. The wool trade centred around the guild of merchants of the Staple of Calais, which was the main marketing and distributive organisation, somewhat similar in function to the Egg or Milk Marketing Boards of today. Thus, the majority of brasses to woolmen are found in the main wool-producing areas—the Cotswolds, the Chilterns and the Lincolnshire Wolds. It is appropriate that three of the London brasses to woolmen are in the Church of All Hallows by the Tower near which lay the medieval wool wharf.

John Field, Alderman of London (1474), was one of the Commissioners appointed to frame regulations for the traffic of wool brought to the Staple of Calais. His effigy bears four shields—the City of London, the merchants of the Staple of Calais, the family coat of arms and, finally, his own trade-mark. His costume is typical of the period—a long gown edged with fur, a leather belt, a gypcière and rosary, and over his shoulders his alderman's gown.

Northleach, in the Cotswolds, possesses the greatest number of wool-merchant brasses to be found in one church—six in all. And probably these burgesses contributed largely to the rebuilding of this magnificent church in the Perpendicular style. Some of the effigies have a sheep at their feet, others have one foot on a sheep and the other on a woolpack.

Comparing the costume of the Northleach wool-staplers with the cassock worn by the clergy to-day, it will be seen that they are nearly identical. The clergy continue to wear the gown which was worn by all civilians four or five centuries ago.

Ecclesiastical figures

Brasses of ecclesiastical figures can be divided into two classes —the secular clergy and the monastic orders. Obviously the majority of these are of priests, but there are also brasses to archbishops and deans, as well as to members of the minor orders of the secular clergy, like doorkeepers and acolytes.

The finest ecclesiastical brass still extant in England is generally considered to be that of Laurence de St. Maur (1337), Rector, at Higham Ferrers, Northants. It is a fine specimen of the brass engraver's art. The vestments, particularly the chasuble, are highly embroidered.

The number of vestments worn by the clergy increased with the rank held, the simple deacon wearing a cassock, the priest covering this with an *alb*, a close-fitting garment, to which are attached six embroidered *apparels* or strips, and the circular chasuble, with a hole for the head, which was draped over the shoulders. The ends of a thin embroidered *stole* are usually visible beneath the chasuble. Archbishops and bishops wore a *rochet*, the double-peaked mitre form of head-dress, knee-length stockings and carried a pastoral staff. Bishop Ysowilpe (1231) at Verden, near Hanover, is a fine Continental example of a bishop in full regalia. Archbishops are seen at New College, Oxford (1417); Chigwell, Essex (1631) and York Minster (1315) and are distinct from bishops in that a Y-shaped pall of white wool is placed over the shoulders hanging both front and back with weighted ends.

On ceremonial occasions, processional vestments were worn. The *cope*, a semi-circular garment, is seen in the canopied brass to Richard de la Barre (1386), a canon who lies buried in Hereford Cathedral. The fleur-de-lys *finials*, or arms, of the octofoil cross in which he is enclosed are repeated on his richly embroidered cope. Sometimes a fur-lined *almuce* or cape-and-hood is seen, although it is often concealed by the cope.

Brasses commemorating abbots, monks and nuns are rare, fig. 14, page 23. When it is remembered that prior to the Reformation, the Church was all-powerful, it is not surprising that the religious upheavals of the sixteenth century found their expression in the destruction of many of its memorials. Abbot Delamare (c. 1360) at St. Albans Abbey is commemorated by a Flemish brass, showing him fully vested with the figures of prophets and Apostles on either side. St. Albans Abbey was formerly a Benedictine monastery and, besides the Delamare brass, contains others of Benedictine monks. Brasses of abbesses and nuns are even rarer, although their apparel is somewhat similar to that of the vowess, described in connection with the costume of widows. At Denham in Bucks is Dame Agnes Jordan

(d. 1540), last abbess of Syon; this is one of the only two brasses of abbesses remaining in England.

Brasses to scholars

University men and graduates appear on a number of brasses in and around Oxford and Cambridge. Many graduates were priests and thus the cassock is the foundation of their dress, over which was worn the gown and cap. As neither colour nor stippling was used to denote the differences in academic habits, it is difficult to distinguish from the costume shown the degrees held by the wearer. However, it has been suggested that a doctor would be represented in rounded cap, fur-lined hood and sleeveless gown with a slit in the front for the hands. Undergraduates, teachers and scholars are rarely depicted on brass. At Wraysbury, Bucks, John Stonor (1512) might be wearing the uniform of an Eton Scholar, although some authorities think that he is depicted as a doctor of law, fig. 22 on page 39.

Brasses to professional men

In contrast to the teaching profession which is centred around the university towns, the legal and administrative professions are fairly widely distributed. The majority of brasses to the legal profession represent judges, whose costume varies very little. The *coif*, a tight-fitting cap, tied beneath the chin, was sometimes covered by a skull cap of black velvet. They also wore a long robe, rather cassock-like, with a fur-lined hooded mantle which was buttoned on the right shoulder. John Cottusmore, Chief Justice of the Common Pleas, at Brightwell Baldwin, Oxon, is typical. The lawyer's tall cap of velvet is seen in the brass to John Edward (1461) at Rodmarton, Glos.

At St. Mary Tower, Ipswich, main centre for the export of cloth during the Middle Ages, are two brasses of notaries. They are represented in normal civilian dress with the pen case of their trade hanging from their belts.

Certain royal officers, heralds and local administrators wear distinctive regalia. Mayors and aldermen wear the civic mantle. Yeomen of the Guard wear the badge of the rose and crown on their doublets.

There are various other types of interesting brasses. However, as these are found all over England and are not merely confined to any particular area they are only mentioned here briefly.

Gruesome brasses

Gruesome brasses are of two types: skeletons and shroud figures. During the middle part of the fifteenth century the commemoration of the dead in their funeral shrouds, or as skeletons, became very popular. Sometimes these were accompanied by inscriptions, intended to put fear into the mind of the beholder: *As ye me see in soche degree so schall ye be anothir day* (1454) Sall, Norfolk. The deceased is usually shown as an emaciated but living body, caught in a shroud which is knotted at both ends.

Garish grinning skeletons are often depicted, an excellent one being that at Margate, engraved in memory of Richard Notfelde (1446). The knowledge of the skeletal structure must have been very limited, for in many instances ribs and vertebrae are not attached to any particular bones but just hang loosely in mid-air.

Sometimes the shroud and skeleton techniques were combined to produce a still more forbidding aspect as, for instance, in the brass to Ralph Hamsterly (c. 1510) at Oddington, Oxon. whose skeleton is swathed in a shroud, with eel-like worms devouring his remains.

Chrysom brasses

During the fifteenth and sixteenth centuries the infant mortality rate was extremely high because of the rigours of childbirth, malnutrition and successive plagues. Infants who died in their first month, before their mother's service of thanksgiving, are shown in swaddling clothes, e.g. Benedict Lee (c. 1520) at Chesham Bois, Bucks.

Chalice and heart brasses

Some pre-Reformation brasses of ecclesiastics, instead of showing the deceased as a complete figure, represent him symbolically in the form of a pair of hands offering a chalice, together with the eucharistic wafer. The majority of such brasses are to be found in Norfolk and Yorkshire.

Bleeding heart brasses are generally reckoned to be symbolic of the heart being buried separately from the rest of the corpse —as an act of reverence for the source of life-blood. John

Merston, Rector of Lillingstone Lovell, Bucks, who died in 1446, is commemorated by a bleeding heart supported by hands. In Oxfordshire, at Caversfield, there is a heart brass inscribed 'credo' (1533). The inscribed 'rose' brass at Edlesborough, Bucks, (1412?) is of the same essence as heart brasses.

Inscriptions

Inscriptions are a secondary aspect of brasses and the letters used are in three kinds of type:

(1) Lombardic, used during the late thirteenth and early fourteenth century and characterized by the easily read and well-formed letters.

(2) Old English or Black Letter; during the fourteenth century this type was characterized by very rounded letters; later it became straighter, more compact and more difficult to read, reverting in the sixteenth century to the original rounded forms which, because they are more extravagant, are known as Tudor style.

(3) Roman Capitals were introduced in the seventeenth century and are very clear to read.

Three languages were used, viz; Norman-French during the thirteenth and fourteenth centuries; Latin and English from the fifteenth onwards.

(1) Norman-French is easily understood with a knowledge of modern French, bearing in mind a few simple axioms, e.g. phonetic spelling, the silent S, the omission of U, and the contraction of words.

(2) Latin inscriptions are more complicated to fathom, abbreviations and omissions occuring frequently, e.g. 'Hic jace(n)t . . .' (Here lie(s) . . .) or 'Or'p'aia' standing for 'Orate pro anima' (Pray for the soul of . . .). The following titles are useful:

Armiger	— esquire	Mercator	— merchant
Capellanus	— chaplain	Miles	— knight
Domina	— dame	Notarius	— notary
Generosus	— gentleman	Sacerdos	— priest
Justiciarus	— justice		

(3) English, used on inscriptions from the fifteenth century onwards, differs considerably from that used nowadays. Chaucer's *Canterbury Tales* provides a good example of the basic dialect and spelling used.

A glossary of words likely to be found on brasses is given in J. Franklyn's book *Brasses*, which includes a chapter on deciphering inscriptions.

So, whereas inscriptions are an ancillary aspect of figure brasses, they are very useful in interpreting the identity and life-span of the person represented and also of dating the costume depicted.

Heraldry

Like inscriptions, armorial bearings are often considered of secondary importance to the main figure brass. However, they play a very important part in the composition of brasses and should by no means be neglected.

Family shields of arms are commonly found let into the slabs towards the corners of the memorial and because of their dissociation from the main brass were often the first pieces to become detached. Needless to say, such shields were engraved very precisely. The terms *dexter* (at the spectator's left) and *sinister* (at the spectator's right) should always be used to describe the positions and component parts of each shield. Enamel colourings were used. *Azure* (blue) and *gules* (red) were extensively employed whilst *sable* (black), *vert* (green) and *purpure* (purple) were less common. Gold, *or* and silver, *argent* were represented by the metals brass and lead respectively.

Crosses and canopies

Like pictures, brasses are in many instances surrounded by a frame, termed a canopy, to set off the main subject. Usually the canopy follows the architectural style of the day.

During the fourteenth century and after, canopies were characterized by tall shafts surmounted by elaborate pinnacles and arches, in the Perpendicular style, fig. 17, page 28. Later, in the second half of the fifteenth century, the gothic style is evident, the arches supporting a frieze, giving the whole a rather cumbersome top-heavy effect.

Cross brasses are of three main types. Simple crosses consist of a plain horizontal shaft (the arms) let into a perpendicular support. The brass ordered in the Basingstoke contract, mentioned on page 6, appears to have been of this type. Some crosses were a variation of this; each arm was terminated by a fleur-delys finial. Floriated crosses were elaborately worked designs, in quatrefoil or octofoil form enclosing a figure of the deceased e.g. Nicholas d'Aumberdene (c. 1350), Taplow, Bucks, fig. 16 on page 28, and Richard de la Barre (1386), a priest, in Hereford Cathedral. Bracket supports to kneeling figures are found on a few brasses.

Pictorial and religious panels

These are to be found on many brasses and are especially interesting where scenes of local places are depicted.

At Bletchley in north Bucks, there is a fine representation of the church, its double towers looming up in the background of a memorial to Dr. Thomas Sparke (1616). In the brass to Robert Braunche (1364) at King's Lynn a peacock feast is depicted, fig. 15 on page 25.

Religious panels showing scenes from the life of Christ are sometimes seen. The crucifixion is depicted in a brass to John Brocas (1492), at Sherborne St. John, Hants. In the brass to Robert Harding (1503) at Cranleigh, Surrey, fig. 20, is a scene of the Resurrection.

Re-used brasses

Brasses which are found to have been appropriated or converted to serve as memorials on a second or subsequent occasion used to be known as palimpsests. However, as this cumbersome term was originally only applied to manuscripts, it is better to call such brasses 're-used'. They are of three types.

Appropriations were brasses that had been removed from their indents or cut from other brasses to serve as memorials to other people. The brass to Ad. Dyxon (1570), at Hampsthwaite, Yorks, is in this category, for it is a fourteenth century brass which had been crudely re-used two centuries later.

A brass was sometimes engraved on one side but then because of an error had to be re-engraved on the other side. These brasses are known as wasters.

Thirdly, many brasses consist of fragments of other brasses, looted from churches in this country and abroad during times of religious persecution, and which were re-engraved to form new memorials on the unused side of the plate. Occasionally this type of re-used brass is mounted so that both sides may be examined, as at Berkhamsted, Herts.

20 Robert Harding, 1503, Cranleigh, Surrey

BRASS RUBBING

The student of brasses often finds it useful to obtain a permanent record of the various brasses he has seen.

The most useful method of procuring a copy is that of brass rubbing, the obtaining of an impression of the brass on paper by rubbing heelball-wax over it.

The materials necessary for brass rubbing are:
1. Detail or lining paper.
2. Heelball.
3. Adhesive or masking tape.
4. Soft brush and rag.

Many brass rubbings lose much of their character because the paper is not wide enough to cover the canopy or inscription. It is important to use a paper of adequate width and weight.

Heelball, suitable for making rubbings, can be obtained from any good quality art shop. The best, made specially for brass rubbing, is obtainable from Phillips & Page Ltd., 50, Kensington Church Street, London, W.8 who can also supply other brass-rubbing requisites.

The brush and cloth should be used for removing grit and dust before starting on the rubbing.

Once you have decided upon a brass to rub it is necessary to obtain permission. It is both courteous and advisable to write to the priest of the church concerned—enclosing a stamped addressed envelope—stating the day you wish to make your rubbing. The address of the incumbent responsible for the upkeep of the church ornaments is to be found in *Crockford's Clerical Directory*, which can be consulted at most local libraries.

Brasses are often situated in awkward positions—on walls, under pews, covered by matting, behind the organ or even outside. The situation of the brass can be ascertained when making enquiries to the priest in charge, who will inform you of its accessibility and whether any fee is payable. Many churches in need of restoration have a box for donations towards the upkeep of the church and its fabric.

Before starting on your rubbing, clean the brass plate carefully with the brush to remove any dust or grit. Roll out the paper on the brass, noting any protruding rivets or faults, and securing it firmly with tape. Then take the cloth and bring out the outline of the brass on the paper by gently feeling for the outline of the plate and indent.

Start rubbing. The most popular technique seems to be to start at the top of the figure and work towards the feet. Brass

21 *Lady, c. 1310, Pitstone,*
   Bucks.

22 *John Stonor, 1512, Wraysbury,*
   Bucks.

rubbing is hard work if a dark even effect is to be obtained. Thus, it is advisable to experiment on a piece of scrap detail paper in order to find the pressure necessary to provide the desired effect. A good way to avoid rubbing over the outline and edges of a figure brass is to use a designer's 'flexi-curve' held firmly as a barrier along the edge to be rubbed.

Where a brass is so detailed that a heelball rubbing is not clear enough, the technique of dabbing may be used. Powdered graphite, obtainable through a chemist, is mixed with raw linseed oil to form a light paste. A pad of chamois leather filled with cotton wool is then moistened with the paste and the effigy is dabbed, a light paper, of tissue quality, being used to obtain a faint grey but fine impression. As dabbing has been known to loosen brasses the incumbent should be consulted first.

Remove the paper, noting any slight mutilations or missing portions to be restored. Where mutilation means that the precise nature of the design cannot be properly determined, only the outline should be filled in, so that the composition of the original is preserved. Polish the finished rubbing with a silk rag before moving and take care to replace any mats or church furniture.

Rubbings can be mounted for decoration on calico or linen-cloth, and hung between wooden laths tapestry-fashion. Shields can be coloured with poster paint. An interesting adaptation of this method is to make a silk-screen print of the rubbing. Facilities for silk-screening exist at local art schools, where evening tuition in the craft is usually available for adults. Another attractive alternative is to make a facsimile colour reproduction of the brass using black or grey paper as a background and a bronze metallic rubber.

The serious student arranges his collection in alphabetical order, labelling rubbings and storing them in cardboard tubes for easy access. A good idea is to photograph a selection of rubbings to save continually handling them.

Collectors may limit their interest to one of many themes—for example, local history, confining their collection to the brasses of one town or county, or, perhaps, Chaucerian or Shakespearean characters—or they can attempt research into engraving workshops by isolating different styles. Where the latter course is preferred, rubbings should be noted with all possible details concerning the memorial. The identity of the deceased, his life history, the situation of the brass in the church, details of missing portions and the heraldic colours of armorial bearings should all be recorded, together with the date rubbed.

OUTSTANDING BRASSES IN BRITAIN

The following lists are for the guidance of persons looking for choice brasses.

Re-used brasses have been excluded because of their general inaccessibility in most instances. Churches possessing brasses of outstanding interest are denoted by an asterisk (*). Serious students are advised to consult a more complete work, such as Mill Stephenson's *List* or the county lists in Macklin's *Monumental Brasses*.

The following abbreviations are used:— C=civilian, E=ecclesiastical figure, M=knight in armour, S=gruesome figure. The total number of brasses in each county is in brackets after each county heading.

BEDFORDSHIRE (121)

Aspley Guise, E 1410. Bromham, M 1435. Cardington, M 1540. Cople, C 1410*. Elstow, E 1524. Marston Moretaine, M 1451. Shillington, E 1400. Wymington, C 1391*, M 1430*. Good selections of brasses are at Ampthill, Cockayne Hatley, Cople, Dunstable and Luton.

BERKSHIRE (140)

Ashbury, C 1360. Bray, M and bracket 1378. Childrey, M 1444*. Shottesbrooke, C and E 1370*. Sparsholt, E in cross 1353*. Wantage, M 1414. West Hanney, E 1370. Windsor, St. George's Chapel, E 1522 (no rubbing). Good selections are at Blewbury, Bray, Childrey, Cookham, Lambourn, Little Wittenham, Sonning (no rubbing), Wantage and West Hanney.

BUCKINGHAMSHIRE (211)

Chenies, C 1510. Denham, E 1540. Drayton Beauchamp, M 1368*; M 1375. Edlesborough, E 1395, rose brass 1412?*. Eton College Chapel, E 1503. Hambleden, C 1500*. Lillingstone Lovell, heart brass 1446*. Middle Claydon, M 1542. Pitstone, C 1310. Quainton, C 1360. Stoke Poges, M 1425. Taplow, C in cross 1350, S 1455. Thornton, M 1472*. Twyford, M 1550. Upper Winchendon, E 1502. Waddesdon, M 1490. Good selections are at Amersham, Burnham, Chalfont St. Giles, Chenies, Denham, Dinton, Eton College Chapel, Penn, Waddesdon and Wooburn.

CAMBRIDGESHIRE (85)

Balsham, E 1401, E 1462*. Burwell, E 1542. Cambridge, St. John's Chapel, E 1414. Cambridge, Trinity Hall, E 1517. Ely Cathedral, E 1554, E 1614. Fulbourn, E 1391. Hildersham, C in cross 1379*; M 1466*, S 1530. Horseheath, M 1365. Isleham, M 1484. Little Shelford, M 1410. Trumpington, M 1289*. Westley Waterless, M 1325*. Wisbech, M 1401. Wood Ditton, M 1393. Good selections are at King's College Cambridge, Fulbourn, Sawston and Little Shelford.

CHESHIRE (7)

Macclesfield, C 1506*. Wilmslow, M 1460*.

CORNWALL (55)

Callington, justice 1465. Lanteglos by Fowey, M 1440. St. Mellion, M 1551. Selections at Crowan, Fowey, Mawgan in Pyder, St. Columb Major and St. Michael Penkivel.

CUMBERLAND (5)

Carlisle, Cathedral, E 1496*. Edenhall, M 1460.

DERBYSHIRE (35)

Dronfield, E 1399. Morley, M 1454, M 1481*. Tideswell, E 1579. Good selections at Hathersage and Morley.

DEVONSHIRE (51)   St Mary of Otterg 1108 (1584)

Dartmouth, St. Saviour, M 1408. Exeter Cathedral, M 1409* (no rubbing), E 1413*. Stoke Fleming, C 1391. Selections at Haccombe and St. Giles-in-the-Wood.

DORSET (29)

Thorncombe, C 1419*. Selections at Caundle Purse, Puddletown and Shapwick.

DURHAM (12)

Auckland, St. Andrew, E 1400. Sedgefield, S 1470, C 1330.

ESSEX (237)

Arkesden, M 1439. Aveley, M 1370*. Bowers Gifford, M 1348? Chigwell, E 1631. Chrishall, M 1370*. Corringham, E 1340. Dagenham, C 1479. Gosfield, C 1440. Great Bromley, E 1432. Latton, M 1467. Little Easton, M 1483*. Little Horkesley, M 1412*, M 1549*. Pebmarsh, M 1323*. Stifford, E 1378. Wimbish, M 1347. Wivenhoe, M 1507*. Good selections are at Barking, Brightlingsea, Clavering, Colchester, Harlow, Hempstead, Hornchurch, Littlebury, Saffron Walden, Stanford Rivers, Tilty, Tolleshunt D'Arcy, Upminster and Writtle.

GLOUCESTERSHIRE (81)

Bristol, St. Mary Redcliffe, M 1475, C 1480. Chipping Campden, C 1401*. Cirencester, M 1438, C 1440*. Deerhurst, judge 1400*. Dyrham, M 1401. Northleach, C 1400*, C 1447*, C 1485*. Rodmarton, lawyer 1461. Wormington, C 1605. Wotton-under-Edge, M 1392*. Good selections of 'woolmen' figure brasses are at Cirencester and Northleach. The fine example at Temple Church, Bristol (1396), was destroyed by enemy action in the last war. Other selections are to be found in Minchinhampton and Fairford.

HAMPSHIRE (69) AND THE ISLE OF WIGHT (6)

Crondall, E 1381. Freshwater, M 1365. Havant, E 1413. Headbourne Worthy, C 1434*. King's Somborne, C 1380. Ringwood, E 1400. Thruxton, M 1425. Winchester, St. Cross, E 1382.

HEREFORDSHIRE (17)

Clehonger, M 1470. Hereford Cathedral, 1290, E 1360, E in cross 1386*, M 1435. Hereford Cathedral has a good varied selection of brasses.

HERTFORDSHIRE (180)

Aldbury, M 1547. Berkhamsted, C 1356*, S 1520. Broxbourne, M 1473. Digswell, M 1415. Furneaux Pelham, C 1420. Hemel Hempstead, M 1390. Hunsdon, C 1495. Knebworth, E 1414. North Mimms, E 1361. St. Albans Abbey, E 1360*. St. Albans—St. Michael, C 1340, C in cross 1400. Sawbridgeworth, M 1433, S 1484, Standon, M 1477. Watford, judge 1415. Watton-at-Stone, M 1361, E 1370. Good selections at Aldenham, Baldock, Berkhamsted, Cheshunt, Clothall, Digswell, Much and Little Hadham, Hitchin, North Mimms, St. Albans Abbey, Sawbridgeworth and Watton-at-Stone.

HUNTINGDONSHIRE (9)

Sawtry, M 1404*. Others at Offord D'Arcy and Diddington.

KENT (330)

Ashford, C 1375. Bexley, hunting horn? 1450. Bobbing, M 1420. Brabourne, M 1433. Chartham, M 1306*. Cobham possesses the finest collection of brasses in England—eighteen dating from 1320 to 1529; (rubbers must apply in advance)***. Dartford, C 1402. East Sutton, M 1629*. East Wickham, C 1325. Faversham, C 1533. Graveney, C 1360*. Herne, M 1430. Hever, M 1538*. Horsmonden, E 1340. Kemsing, E 1347. Lydd, C 1430. Maidstone, C 1593. Margate, C 1431, S 1446. Mereworth, M 1366? Minster in Sheppey, M 1330*. Northfleet, E 1375*. Saltwood, M 1437; angel and heart 1496*. Seal, M 1395. Sheldwich, M 1394. Ulcombe, M 1419. Upper Hardres, E and bracket 1405*. Woodchurch, E in cross 1330. Wrotham, M 1532. Good selections are at Addington, Ash next Sandwich, Biddenden, Birchington, Canterbury, Chartham, Cobham, Dartford, Erith, Faversham, Great Chart, Herne, Hever, Hoo St. Werburgh, Lydd, Margate, Newington-next-Hythe, Pluckley, Southfleet, Westerham (no rubbing), and Wrotham.

LANCASHIRE (17)

Childwall, M 1524. Ormskirk, M 1500. Sefton, M 1568*, M 1570. Winwick, M 1492*; M with chasuble 1527*. Selections of brasses are at Manchester Cathedral and Middleton.

LEICESTERSHIRE AND RUTLAND (26) (4)

Bottesford, E 1404*. Castle Donington, M 1458. Little Casterton, M 1410. Sibson, E 1532. Stockerston, M 1467. Wanlip, M 1393*.

LINCOLNSHIRE (84)

Barton upon Humber, St. Mary, C 1433. Boston, C 1398*, E 1400. Broughton, M 1390. Buslingthorpe, M 1300. Croft, M 1300. Grainthorpe, cross 1380, Gunby, C 1419. Irnham, M 1390. Linwood, C 1419*. Scrivelsby, M 1545. Spilsby, C 1391, M 1410. Stamford, All Saints, 2 woolmen 1465. Tattershall, M 1456, C 1470, E 1510. Good selections are at Tattershall and at Boston, where there are also many incised slabs.

CENTRAL LONDON (say 50)

All Hallows by the Tower, woolman 1437, C 1533. St. Dunstan-in-the-West, C 1530. Westminster Abbey, E 1395, E 1399*, M 1437.

Good selections are at All Hallows by the Tower, St. Giles, Camberwell, St. Helen's, Bishopsgate and Westminster Abbey.

OUTER LONDON (say 70)

Enfield, C 1470*. Fulham, C 1529. Harrow, M 1390, E 1468. Hillingdon, M 1509. Wandsworth, C 1420. Good selections are at Hackney, Hadley, Harefield, Harrow, Hillingdon, Ruislip and Willesden, St. Mary's.

MONMOUTHSHIRE (5)

Mathern, C 1590. Usk, inscription in Welsh, 1400.

NORFOLK (215)

Aylsham, S 1499. Blickling, M 1401. Bylaugh, M 1471. Elsing, M 1347*. Fakenham, 4 hearts 1500. Felbrigg, M and C 1380; M 1416*. Holme-next-the-Sea, C 1405. Hunstanton, M 1506*. Ketteringham, M 1499. King's Lynn, C 1349*, C 1364*. Methwold, M 1361. Narborough, C 1545. Norwich, St. George Colegate, C and bracket, 1472; St. John Maddermarket, C and bracket, 1524; St. Lawrence, E 1437. Reepham, M 1391. Rougham, M 1472. Southacre M 1384*. Upwell, E 1430. Good selections of brasses are at Aldeborough, Aylsham, Bawburgh, Blickling, Cley, Felbrigg, Frenze, Loddon, Narborough, Necton and in the churches of Norwich where a number of 'gruesome' brasses are to be seen.

NORTHAMPTONSHIRE (106)

Ashby St. Ledgers, M 1494. Brampton-by-Dingley, M 1420. Castle Ashby, E 1401. Charwelton, C 1490. Cotterstock, E and bracket, 1420. Easton Neston, M 1552. Greens Norton, M 1462. Higham Ferrers, E 1337**, C 1425, E 1498. Lower Heyford, M 1487. Lowick, M 1467. Newton-by-Geddington, C 1400. Rothwell, E 1361. Good selections of brasses are at Ashby St. Ledgers, Higham Ferrers***, Wappenham and Warkworth.

NORTHUMBERLAND (2)

Newcastle-upon-Tyne, C 1429* (no brass rubbing).

NOTTINGHAMSHIRE (12)

Clifton, M 1478, M 1491, M 1587. East Markham, C 1419. Holme Pierrepont, C 1380. Newark, C 1361*. Strelley, M 1487. Wollaton, M 1471. Fair selection of brasses and inscriptions at Newark.

OXFORDSHIRE (235)

Brightwell Baldwin, judge 1439*. Broughton, C 1414. Burford, C and bracket, 1437. Caversfield, heart brass 1435. Checkendon, C 1404. Chinnor, M 1385. Dorchester, E 1510. Great Tew, M 1410. Mapledurham, M 1395. Oddington, S 1510*. Oxford, Merton College Chapel, E 1322, E and bracket, E 1471. New College Chapel, E 1417*. Rotherfield Greys, M 1387. Thame, M 1420, M 1460. Good selections are at Chinnor, Chipping Norton (no rubbing), Dorchester, Harpsden, Oxford, Christchurch Cathedral, Magdalen College, Merton College Chapel, New College Chapel, Queen's College Chapel and Thame.

SHROPSHIRE (16)
Acton Burnell, M 1382*. Adderley, E 1390. Edgmond, S 1533. Harley, M 1475. Tong, M 1467*.

SOMERSET (44)
Ilminster, M 1440*, M 1618. South Petherton, M 1430. There are interesting brasses at Wells Cathedral and Yeovil.

STAFFORDSHIRE (15)
Audley, M 1385*. Horton, C 1589. Norbury, C 1360. Okeover, M 1447. Standon, cross brass 1450.

SUFFOLK (215)
Acton, M 1302*. Barsham, M 1415. Burgate, M 1409. Gorleston, M 1320. Ipswich, Museum C 1525, St. Mary Tower, 2 notaries. Letheringham, M 1389. Long Melford, C 1420. Mendlesham, M 1417. Playford, M 1400*. Stoke by Nayland, M 1408. Yoxford, S 1485. Good selections are at Acton, Aldeburgh, Brundish, Euston, Ipswich St. Mary Tower, Little Bradley, Little Waldingfield, Long Melford, Orford, Sotterley, Stoke by Nayland and Yoxford.

SURREY (130)
Beddington, C 1432, M 1437. Carshalton, M 1485. Crowhurst, M 1450. East Horsley, E 1478. Horley, C 1420. Lingfield, M 1403 (no rubbing), C 1374. Oakwood, M 1431 (under glass). Stoke d'Abernon, M 1277***, M 1327**. Good selections are at Beddington, Bletchingley, Carshalton, Cheam, East Horsley, Lingfield, Merstham, Shere, Stoke d'Abernon and Thames Ditton.

SUSSEX (110)
Amberley, M 1424. Ardingly, C 1500. Battle, vice-chancellor of Oxford 1615*. Broadwater, cross 1445. Buxted, E in cross 1408. Cowfold, E 1433**. Etchingham, M 1388, M 1444. Fletching, M 1380. Hurstmonceux, M 1402. Trotton, C c.1310**, M 1419*. West Grinstead, C 1440*. Wiston, M 1426. Good selections of brasses at Ardingly, Arundel Castle chapel, Battle, Stopham, and West Firle.

WARWICKSHIRE (51)
Baginton, M 1407. Merevale, M 1413. Warwick St. Mary, M 1406*. Wixford, M 1411. Brasses at Compton Verney House are inaccessible. Selections of brasses at Coleshill, Upper Schuckburgh and Tredington.

WESTMORLAND (4)
Great Musgrave, E 1500.

WILTSHIRE (47)
Clyffe Pypard, M 1380. Dauntsey, C 1539. Draycot Cerne, M 1393. Mere, M 1398. Salisbury Cathedral, E in castle 1375*, E 1578*. Bromham and Tisbury have good selections of brasses.

WORCESTERSHIRE (27)
Fladbury, M 1445. Kidderminster, M 1415*. The latter has a good selection of brasses.

YORKSHIRE (66)

Aldborough, M 1360* (no rubbing). Allerton Mauleverer, M. 1400. Beeford, E 1472. Brandesburton, M 1397*. Cottingham, E 1383. Cowthorpe, judge 1494. Harpham, M 1418*, M 1445. Ripley, chalice brass, 1429. Topcliffe, C 1391*. Wensley, E 1360*. York Minster, E 1315 (no rubbing). Good selections of small brasses and inscriptions are to be found in the old churches of the city of York and also at Doncaster, Ilkley, Leeds, Ripon, Sheffield and Wath.

WALES (say 50)

Anglesey: Beaumaris, C 1530.
Caernarvon: Dolwyddelan, M 1535. Llanbeblig, C 1500.
Denbigh: Llanrwst, 6 civilian brasses, 1620-1671 (no rubbing).
Glamorgan: Swansea, C 1500.
Montgomery: Bettws, Newtown, E 1531.
Pembroke: Pembroke C 1654. St. David's M (Victorian replacement of brass of Edmund Tudor).

SCOTLAND (4)

Aberdeen, St. Nicholas, C 1613. Glasgow, Cathedral, M 1605. In Dunfermline Abbey there is a modern brass erected in memory of Robert the Bruce (1274-1329); it is executed in the style of the late thirteenth century and is surrounded by an inscription in Latin.

IRELAND (5)

Mural brasses at St. Patrick's and Christchurch cathedrals.

Many museums and local archaeological societies have collections of rubbings which may be examined. However, as the majority of these collections are not readily accessible, it is advisable to make enquiries before starting out.

Victoria and Albert Museum, South Kensington, S.W.7.

Ask for the "Print Room" which is open 10 a.m.-5 p.m. on weekdays. The collection is arranged according to costume and date.

British Museum, Bloomsbury, W.C.1.

You should proceed to the Department of Manuscripts, where the collections of the pioneer authorities on brasses are kept. Temporary daily-admission passes are issued to persons genuinely interested in specific rubbings listed in the Department's catalogues.

Society of Antiquaries of London, Burlington House, W.1.

Write, asking for permission to view on a specified date between 10 a.m. and 5 p.m. This collection, kept in large folders, is topographically arranged and is the most complete of all.

Other collections are held by the Museum of Archaeology and Ethnology, Cambridge; The Ashmolean Museum, Oxford; Northampton Architectural Society; St. Peter Hungate Museum, Norwich, the Surrey Archaeological Society, Guildford; the Metropolitan Museum, New York and the Smithsonian Museum, Washington, D.C.

Many of these institutions also possess single brasses and fragments and their collections are especially valuable to the researcher as they include rubbings of brasses which are no longer extant.

The Monumental Brass Society

The Monumental Brass Society was founded in 1887 for the preservation and study of brasses, indents and incised slabs. Each year it publishes a portfolio of plates and an issue of Transactions as well as holding meetings. Membership is open to any person genuinely interested and further particulars may be obtained from Honorary Secretary, Monumental Brass Society, c/o Society of Antiquaries, Burlington House, Piccadilly, London W.1.

Titles in paperback in the 'Discovering' series:

Abbeys and Priories 25p
American Story in England 25p
Antique Firearms 25p
Antique Maps 30p
Archaeology in England/Wales 25p
The Bath Road 22½p
Battlefields in N. England and
    Scotland 22½p
Battlefields in Southern England 25p
Bells and Bellringing 25p
Berkshire 17½p
The Birmingham Road 22½p
Brasses and Brass Rubbing 25p
Bridges 25p
British Postage Stamps 30p
Buckinghamshire 17½p
The Bucks Explorer 17½p
Burford 20p
Canals 25p
Carts and Wagons 25p
Castle Combe 12½p
Castles in Central England 25p
Castles in Eastern England 25p
Cathedrals 30p
Chesham 17½p
Cheshire 30p
Christmas Customs & Folklore 25p
Church Furniture 25p
Civic Heraldry 25p
Coins 25p
Crosses 30p
Devon 17½p
Dorset 15p
East Suffolk 12½p
Embroidery 30p
England's Trees 25p
English County Regiments 25p
English Customs 30p
English Fairs 25p
English Furniture 1500-1720 25p
English Furniture 1720-1830 30p
English Gardens 22½p
Essex 30p
The Exeter Road 22½p
Flower Arrangement 22½p
Folklore in Industry 22½p
The Folklore of Plants 30p
The Gloucester Road 22½p
Gloucestershire 22½p
Hallmarks on English Silver 25p
Hampshire 22½p
Herbs 25p
Hertfordshire 25p
High Wycombe 17½p
Highwaymen 25p
Horse Brasses 22½p
Inn Signs 25p

Leicestershire 22½p
Lincolnshire 30p
London for Children 30p
London—Off-beat Walks 25p
London Railway Stations 30p
London Statues & Monuments 25p
Lost Theatres 30p
Mermaids and Sea Monsters 17½p
Militaria 25p
Military Traditions 25p
Model Soldiers 25p
Northamptonshire 22½p
Oxfordshire 17½p
Picture Postcards 25p
Place-names 25p
Regional Archaeology—
    Central England 30p
    Cotswolds & Upper Thames 30p
    Eastern England 30p
    North-Eastern England 30p
    North-Western England 30p
    South-Western England 30p
    Wessex 30p
The Road to the Costa Brava 22½p
The Road to Provence 22½p
The Road to Rome/Florence 22½p
The Road to Rome/Genoa 22½p
The Road to Salzburg 22½p
The Road to Venice 22½p
Saints in Britain 22½p
Sea Shells 30p
Smoking Antiques 22½p
Spas 30p
Staffordshire Figures 30p
Stained Glass 25p
Statues Central & N. England 25p
Statues in Southern England 25p
Surnames 22½p
Surrey 17½p
This Old House 25p
Topiary 25p
Towns 22½p
Traction Engines 25p
Trade Tokens 30p
Wall Paintings 25p
Wargames 25p
Warwickshire 17½p
Watermills 25p
Windmills 22½p
Windsor 25p
The Wines of Madeira 17½p
Wrought Iron 25p
Yorkshire—moors and coast 25p
Your Family Tree 30p
Zoos, Bird Gardens and Animal
    Collections 25p

*From your bookseller or from Shire Publications, Tring, Herts.
(Please add 3p postage and packing)*

Printed by Maund & Irvine Ltd., Tring, Herts.